The Joyful Dark

The Joyful Dark

Poems by

Michael Miller

The Ashland Poetry Press
Ashland University
Ashland, Ohio 44805

Some of these poems have appeared previously in the following publications:

The American Scholar, "Last Love"
The Carolina Quarterly, "At Longfellow's House"
The Centennial Review, "White Owl"
Commonweal, "A Marble Stockpile"
Crosscurrents, "Leafing Out"
Hawaii Review, "Buckets"
International Poetry Review, "Dogwood"
The Kenyon Review, "First Kingdom"
The Literary Review, "Nightmare"
Manhattan Poetry Review, "Red-Wing"
The New Republic, "Procession"
Pacific Review, "Hummingbird"
The Pennsylvania Review, "Crow"
Poetry East, "Natural History 3"
Poetry Now, "Shark"
The Seattle Review, "Young Whales"
The Sewanee Review, "The Steel-Backed Boys"
The South Dakota Review, "Stations"
The Southern Review, "The Photograph"
Southwest Review, "The Nesting Box"
The Texas Review, "Fulton Street"
The Yale Review, "The Old Lovers"

"White Owl" appeared in the *Anthology of Magazine Verse & Yearbook of American Poetry*: 1986-1988 edition.

Some poems first appeared in the limited edition chapbooks: *Jackhammer* (Helikon Press) and *Leafing Out* (Finishing Line Press).

Credit for cover photo and author photo: Mary Miller

Printed in the United States of America

ISBN-10: 0–912592–62–1
ISBN-13: 978–0–912592–62–6

Library of Congress Catalog Card Number: 2007936917

for Mary

Contents

V

VI

I

Bones

1.

On the green steel of its legs
The praying mantis, the female,
Rises above the male
After he has driven into her
And they have joined for a moment,
Then bites off his head.

2.

Not love, but lust only
Draws us into the grass
Where your muscular legs
Lock me into a vise
As I imagine snapping your neck
And cradling your head
Which I begin to eat slowly.

3.

I devour you to become you,
To breathe in your marrow
And flow through your blood
Until the rot clinging to my body
Falls away like an old scab
And I feast on the purity of bones.

4.

On the long yellow grass
Stiff as the bristles of an old broom
Your naked body lies

Asleep in the folds of the dark,
While I, leaving in silence,
Enter the woods to hunt.

5.

I push the torn flesh together,
Sealing the skin flaps
As a thin line of blood
Edges around each bite,
Using my fingers, my tongue,
Wondering what animal
Feasted on your sleeping body?

6.

What I have tried to destroy,
What I have seized with the heart
Of the hunter, you have released,
Offering yourself to the wind
With invisible wings that
Beat through my dreams.

7.

Uncaptured, you move further away,
Leaving my hands empty,
Allowing me to fill the space
With a stranger
Clad in your furry body.

8.

I still remember the ugly
Unwashed bodies that moved

So awkwardly in my bed,
Leaving gold teeth and tattoos
In my dreams and dark blood
On the sheets which I am
Still trying to wash away.

9.

And if you choose return,
If you can see beyond
My deceptions, my cruelty,
I will amputate my hands
And love you with my stumps
That have never touched another.

10.

Beyond lust we lie,
Our bodies spent, our hands
Folded upon our chests,
Our hips touching like stones
That have been smoothed
By years of rubbing together.

Among the Gravestones

On this winter's night
Rinsed by the cold moon's glare
An old memory quarrels
In my thoughts as we lie down
In search of sleep and peace.
I remember a pondside graveyard
On a hill of grassy earth
That climbed into the sun
As we stood beneath a willow's
Swaying tassels, watching the water
As the swans came suddenly,
Ominous ugly swans
Threatening the air
With knobbed orange bills,
Dingy thrashing wings and loud
Racketing cries that drove us back
Among the gravestones with
Faded names and blurs for dates.
"Dempsey, Hastings, McCallum!"
You shouted, throwing names
And syllables at the swans
Until the hissing birds
Fled back to water and we stood
In silence, our perfect day
Disrupted by that menace of swans
That bore no trace of beauty.
Now I look at you asleep
In sheets like folded wings
With hair pressed down like feathers,
And move again toward love's uncertainties,
Toward love's startling surprises.

Single Moon

I move across your single moon of breast
To that empty space I turned away from once,
Desiring you complete, unscarred, without the
Ravishment begun by the grinding jaws of crab.
Now we speak of beauty and defilement, how disease
Can ravage what we cherish, how portions of the body
Can decay, how we, like plants susceptible to sudden
Growths of fungus, can change within an hour, a day.
I see you with young lilies, kneeling on the damp
Dark earth, accepting your disfigurement as a part
Of life, a part of death, and caring for the lilies,
Fair interlopers of continual arrival, departure.

Not the Beautiful

It is not the daffodils, yellow as
A young girl's long hair that matter,
Nor is it the fullness of the red tulips
Opening like mouths waiting to be kissed,
Nor anything else in the garden
That you brought into being
And is now as beautiful as the streaks
Of pink that stretch like ribbons
Across the early morning sky.
It is not the beautiful that matters
But who creates it, what they gave to it.
It was their intention, their labor
That matters, not the flowers that wilt,
Not the petals that fall and shrivel
Like torn letters left in the rain.

Bluet

The bluet grows in clusters
At the corners of the field,
Its yellow heart like drops
Of sunlight that refuse to set,
Like love that grows resilient
In the tug of war of marriage.
When you bend to look
You become the bluet,
Your fingers, the petal's trembling,
Your breath its blue perfection
In the greenhouse of the spring.

Portrait

So peacefully across the vistas
Of the mind the simple images recur:
A spoon-shaped lake, a picnic table,
A family with baskets walking on
The mats of yellowed grass,
Moving past us with an old woman
Trailing at a hazy distance,
Her hair as white as porcelain
And her wrinkles gathering the shadows
Waiting in the air.
Then the man with gentled hands
Settled her beneath the branches
Of a ninety-year-old silver maple
Which she leaned against
Without a word, without a gesture,
Surrendered to the silence of the leaves
As the darting warblers
Drew purple threads across the trees.
We watched this family of summer,
Letting thoughts of age and death
Drift by us like the leaves
Already floating on the lake,
And what I felt was love,
Love translated into images
Taking residence in a place
Beyond the vows we made,
And then you said, "When I grow old
Put me under the trees."

II

Natural History

1.

Dreaming, seized by a praying mantis,
The clean jaw of death, cold
As a razor, I shout, wake,
And press against you,
A trembling leaf falling
To earth.

2.

By the sleeping river
We felt the current breathe:
The sunfish, clustered like stars,
Glided past an old crab
Scuttling among rocks.
Our son, small as a tadpole,
Stirred within you.

3.

White, geometrical, a graveyard
Of funnels, pipes, electric fences,
The plant glows with sterility,
A nuclear child riveted like a man's
Bad dream. Shutting my eyes,
I invent pastures.

4.

After the words, the syllable bullets,
The tension sizzling like a fuse,
We return to silence,

The first understanding of flesh.
Weary, our bodies braided,
We sleep long.

5.

Thumping toward birth,
Somersaulting in the amniotic sea,
Our son defies the dark,
Kicking through dreams, hiccuping,
While you, sleeping mother,
Cover your stomach, linking your arms
Like chains.

6.

And the fetal monitor resounded
With the beating of an unborn heart
And the slow drip of pitocin
Speeded the laboring uterus' contractions
And the flesh spread from the episiotomy
And the head emerged like a blue flower's bulb
And a wet dog-paddling boy
Slithered through a pulsing door.

7.

After the birth,
After the spongy placenta ripped,
The clots poured like roses:
The uterus, shrinking, crept
To its cave deep in the pelvis,
And you, gently, cradled the child.

14

8.

I touch his head,
Ridged like a walnut:
Unformed bone, knot of skull,
Soft cleft like a thumbprint
In a peach that allows
His brain to grow.

9.

Half asleep, your belly
A deflated balloon,
You nurse our son, his tiny mouth
Working steadily, like an old man
Gumming bread, sucking sweetness
From the pale milk.

10.

Our son sleeps, as though unborn,
His hand rises, falls,
A five-streamered kite without string:
The leaves drift, decay;
Columbia orbits the earth, a gyroscope
Of shadow; our son sucks,
The world in his thumb.

11.

The body changes, the man I was
Drifts through my dreams,
Drawing me to places without names,
To evenings by the sea where the sandpiper
Skims the water's ruffled rim
And you, a figure out of shadow,

Come to me through dunes and dark,
Bearing bowls of mongrel flowers,
Tigerish flowers that fall
Like burning lace.

12.

Our autumn child,
His long body rising like a mast,
His hands flapping like sails,
Prepares for voyages,
And we, moored ships
In a deep harbor,
Rock with the waves,
Sing to the tides.

Leafing Out

Leafing out, shrugging
Through wind, the sycamore
Bursts into spring, pushing
Through frost, discarding
The snow like an old man
Leaving a coat.

Beneath its branches,
Like blind seekers feeling
Their way, we stroke the bark,
The history of scars,
The imperfections we learn
To embrace, to endure.

Marred and no longer young,
Twisted together
After a quarrel with years,
We felt our wounds
Bring forth a child,
An unblemished son.

First Kingdom

Where the cross-eyed green-striped tiger
Laughs at the blue bear
The size of a stuffed woolen sock,
We meet, a child, a man,
Both wanderers in the first kingdom
Where Little Bo-peep, singing, swaying,
Follows her sheep, and you,

Gregory, my son with the sprouting locks,
With flesh as fine as the down of roses,
Discover friendship with the animals,
The sewn creatures of silence and smiles
Who share your playpen world
Of trees, wildflowers, and jungles
Of crepe paper leaves.

And now you turn, you stare,
Your three-months-old eyes brighten
Like marbles of night
While your inch of hand waves
Like a welcoming pennant of peace
And your tiny bunched body bundled with warmth
Melts frosted windows,

Asking to touch before you trust,
And if I, a friendly giant
Entering your garden,
Could step inside the softness
Of your widening eye
I would rock with the red rocking-horse
And be as merry as Old King Cole.

But I, a renegade in the world
Where rhyme must have reason,
Where love is a word dealt out in spades
And the shuffle of sex disorders the soul,

Must come to you with a peddler's sack
Of forgotten songs, bearing no promises,
No prophecies, no gold leafed pages,

But in other worlds, in other lands
Where stars fall instead of satellites,
We can still follow the blue bear,
The cross-eyed green-striped tiger,
And the sheep who baa
As they lead us, and keep us,
In the vanishing spaces of love.

The Nesting Box

The house-bound days, a wife, a child,
A marriage of order, faded like dreams
As I climbed the cow-pied pasture,
The clumpy hill mushroomed with stones
Where maples swayed like brushes of fire
And red-tailed hawks plummeted down
The slides of the wind, and there,
A stranger to wildness, the hawk's domain,
I found a wooden nesting box,
A vertical coffin nailed to a stake
Of solitary pine, its dark eye
Drawing me like a tunnel. And then,
As curious as a child, I lifted up
The heavy lid, expecting layers of grass,
But sprawled across the narrow bottom
A dead sparrow lay, its wings spread
Like a shredded kite, its tiny head
Scratched like an aging wedding band.
We enter things we cannot leave,
But love, an uncaged hawk, lifts us
Over the invisible fences of marriage.

Intruder

Some would call the police
At the sight of his massive body
Prowling through the night,
Past the windows, by the porch,
Until he stops, rises, and grasps
The bird-feeder between his claws,
Eating the seed as fireflies flash
Warnings across the waves of dark.
But we step softly out the door
To watch him eat: black bear
Beneath the sky's blind eye;
And we move closer, closer,
And begin to love our fear.
He is gone before we know it,
Leaving scattered seed,
This dark intruder who passed
At midnight through our quiet lives
To give us what we needed.
We close the door, undress together,
And make love without a word.
We feel his presence in the room,
Above our bodies, exciting us.

III

Buckets

When the blackberry bush
Refuses to fatten
I search for buckets
That hang on the trunks
Of sugar maples.
For days, for years,
My body remembers: the distance
Stretching between trees,
The fences of snow.
But when darkness thickens
Like a pool of sap,
When the rootless dead push
Toward the path in the eye
Of all blossoms, I hurry
Until my scarred paws
Reach toward the buckets.
Nobody knows how much I eat
To keep alive.

Dogwood

Beyond a cluster of cherry trees
Whose scarfs of blossom
Brighten the night
The stalwart dogwood stands,
Gnarled, twisted, but blooming,
Struggling into spring.

Despite its trunk of scar,
Its broken, rotting branches,
The aged dogwood sways in shadow,
Surrendering to wind, to rain,
And shrugging off the birds of hunger,
The stabbing beaks, striking talons,

The moonlit tree bows down,
Drinking from the cups of earth,
Receiving yet extending,
Offering its limbs, its leaves,
Its knots of blossom,
Part of the light, part of the dark.

Aviary

Crow

His wings bent like boomerangs,
The printed directions of stars locked
In his blood, the crow turns toward earth.

Outside our opened window, on a swaying
Branch of silver maple, he perches,
Fixed on the moon, the nest of stars.

You, crow, truculent masculine bird
Screeching into the mute sky's indifference,
Enter our window, eat from our hands.

Red-Wing

Unmistakable, no tanager,
Bobolink, or boat-tailed grackle,
But a breeder in marshes,
A high-pitched singer
With epaulets bright as the sky's
Red eye, he flies from cattails,
Skimming the marsh where herons
Draw in their wings like cloaks.
Without a mate, without a nest,
He pauses on reeds, willows,
And swamp magnolias,
Snatches a worm, swallows a berry.
Alone, high on a branch,
He calls, he waits.

Mallard

After sunset, on the still marsh
Where blades of ice push together,
A mallard's torn wing flapped like a rag,
His neck arched, glossed like an emerald.

Beyond rescue, the duck screeched
"Yeeb-yeeb!" summoning the blind stars,
The sickle moon, the night shadows
Passing like claws over branches.

No help, no reply. Only silence,
Sleepwalking ice surrounding the mallard,
Devouring his island of water,
Confining his breast, his frantic feet.

At sunrise, I crossed the bank,
The frozen marsh, and saw the head,
Erect, twisted, his mad eyes fixed,
Glaring in a guillotine of ice.

Cardinal

Flame-crested,
The cardinal surveys
His green domain,
Allows no marauders,
Beak ready to strike,
A straight stab
From a small god.

I watched him chase
A hooligan crow across
An invisible map of sky,
Defending his territory,
Refusing to relinquish
An inch of what instinct
Dictates is his.

Hummingbird

And wings like blurred water
Startle me, then the hum,
The iridescent throat,
The suspended metallic body
Shuddering over roses,
A transient messenger
Disturbing the silence.
Untethered, a pine-needle bill
Cutting south from Saskatchewan,
A fork-tailed seeker
Drawn to the throat of flowers,
This hummingbird
Lifts me from the stupor
Of summer, the heaviness
Of marriage, the stone
Weighing down love.

White Owl

Past carriages of bone,
Cobweb stars and sleeves
Of snakeskin, high in the rafters
Of the burnt-out barn
I found a scraggly white owl,
Its flattened face
Pressed like a foxglove
On a page, its talons
Peeling like the bark
Of aging golden birches,
And staring at its eyes,
So watchful, so alive,
So far beyond death's symbol,
I thought of you: old love,
Old vows, enduring still.

Shark

Shovel-headed, glass-eyed, unhurried
In his hugeness, prowling beneath the
Smooth wave's shoulder, he glides toward
The corrupted heaven of the swimmers
Kicking through his brackish door.
Cold-nosed, thick skinned, a scavenger
But no sea brute, he swallows distance,
Darting through the greenery of dark,
Alone, aloof, graceful as a cutting blade,
And in his kingdom of blood-streaked blue,
Sanctified by centuries, by instinct
Innocent of greed, ignorant of cruelty,
He reigns supreme, imperishable,
The mute impartial killer of the sea.

Young Whales

Warm-blooded, air-breathing, the young whales
Feed off their mother's milk, then turn, lobtailing
Into the sea's blue acres, diving deeply toward
A shipwreck's skeleton, a galleon of bones.
Here their world begins. They announce themselves
With songs, high-pitched frequencies of sound
That carry through blue distances in untutored
Fields of dream. Bodied forth in a country
Without men, furrowing the salt-sown pastures
Of their mother's wake, oblivious of Aristotle's
First description and Pliny's sea-monster myths,
These whales overturn no vessel but frolic
Through the blue meadows of undersea spring.
In gentle kingdoms their huge brains cannot imagine
The hanging shadows of whalers or the high-powered
Harpoons bulleting through the sea's calm surface.

Half Born

On a hillside, two lambs rest,
Their eyes drawing them down to dream,
To the body of their half born brother
Drowning in the eye of birth yolk,
Curled like crimson tissue
In the slippery world of the womb's
Blue-black water: who followed
Their kicking bodies but stopped;
His body limp, his will-less life
Ignoring his mother's bumping nose.
Somewhere they remember, his hour
Of struggle, his ease in death.

IV

If Men Could Have Babies

If men could have babies
And lovely ladies swung hammers
Toward the stars,
Each dumbstruck morning
Would scatter the driving seed
And binding ghosts
Of roaring Jack and gentle Jill
Would mourn empty notes
From crumpled horns.

No longer would golden girls
Dance dreams of love
Or limber boys
Pick bursting buds,
But in sea-sliding darkness
Curving stems would stretch
To headstrong tides.
Men follow the female strut
Or stand alone and die.

The Steel-Backed Boys

Summer locks the steel-backed boys
Of spring in sweat, their midday feasts
Drink seas of passion, and shores
Of sorrow are swept by tides of sun.
These boys, shameless boys who seek
The seeds of song, forget their blindness
That forces failure and dooms the day.
Now they shout, their sporting friends
Are fathers of their folly, their winter
Wounds are worthy of more wine, and each
Finds his heart in heaven's hollow,
Leaping toward the burning skin of stars.

Demon

How many deaths must she die
Before she is dead,
This woman I call mother
Who reigns over my dreams,
Rousing me in a night sweat?
I stalk her like a hunter
Its prey, driven by the demon
Of unattainable love,
Looking toward light
Edging over the hills,
Hoping this dawn may bring
An end to her deaths.

Nightmare

I wake and watch my bones
Grow old, my father locks an
Iron door, my mother screams,
My brother whispers in a shroud,
My sister hides in closets,
Her gentle hands are strong.

Vengeance shouts "Stand up!"
My shrunken eyes begin to see,
I hunt the narrow hollows
Where shadows wind around
Themselves, I fight for breath
And chase the madman's sex.

Every kiss embraces death,
Each slippery body shimmers
Like a blue-skinned boy,
A hooded face streams with
Blood, my hands find scars
Instead of love.

A knot of roses binds my feet,
Petals, thorns, blanket my bed.
Who wanders through my dreams
And softly dislocates my sex?
My breastless mother weeps,
Her eyes glow like mascara moons.

Turning outward like a child,
I advance without protection.
Darkness leafs through the sky,
Silent hands undress the trees.
I hear the moon whisper and see
The sun practice how to die.

How free it feels to breathe!
To lift my head and stride
Beyond this night of mutes,
To live each day by dying,
Through the summer's whimsy
And the frozen hands of snow.

But why are faces hardened,
Like leaves that dry, crack,
And crumble? What mirror still
Reflects the birth of carnage?
The mind breaks down the body,
Blood freezes into thought.

V

Manhattan Island

A digging city burying its beginning,
Exhaling the traffic of confusion.
Cement twists, pile-drivers cough,
The pulse of jackhammers
Buckles the street.
Alone on a crowded corner,
Feeling the city's pounding echo,
I meet you, dear friend,
In a softer, safer world.

The Photograph

Roof gutters, gargoyles, a narrow
Street with shadows leaning down
The backs of cobblestones, and you,
Capturing a place through a camera's eye.
Flattened, imprisoned behind glass,
Your photograph, the rue St.-Louis-
En-L'Ile, endures the changing light
And shift of years. You, traveler,
At home in foreign lands; I, whitening
Toward winter with a different life,
Never to meet except in memory's shade.
I stare into the shapes, the shadows,
The photograph you took is you.

Stations

Between ramps, baggage carts,
Changing faces shuttling through
The musky tunnels of track,
The sleepwalking engines gliding
Past Toronto, Albany, Hudson County,
I waited, imagining your appearance
In the ominous, arched corridors
Of Grand Central Station.

Travelers debark, bodies threaten
My path, and the thought of death,
Authoritative as the voice of
The stationmaster, enters my spirit
Like a scalpel's fine incision.
All stations, Victoria, Gare du Nord,
Attend the journey, the traveler
Seeking his land, his likeness.

A Marble Stockpile

Between Second Avenue and Third
On 37th Street, a cold day
In a converted stable,
A marble stockpile!
And you beside me,
Before brick walls
And potbellied stoves,
Walking between cut machines,
Steel-eyed drills, diamond wheels,
And all the while,
As though asleep and awake,
I drifted in time, passing
Florentine and Norwegian Rose,
Recalling Donatello, Michelangelo,
Canova, until suddenly
You rose before me,
Set apart from steel blue clarity,
Contrasted between gray flats,
White slates and marble dust,
Your eyes clear,
Your skin translucent,
And for a moment I held you,
Ageless in time,
Until you trembled.
Marble endures.

Fulton Street

A deserted market with scales
Hanging from iron chains,
With crabs of shadow, dripping
Walls of net, with you, me,
Weary figures walking toward
Dawn, past creaking gates,
Spoon-necked gulls, a barnacled
Pier which held our bodies.
We slept as naked children,
Waking in each other's dream.

At Longfellow's House

The young wife who courted fire
Reached for the glowing candle,
Sealing strands of hair into a golden locket.
Suddenly a flame snaked up
Her muslin sleeve, a dancing torch
Streaked through the shuttered house,
And running toward her husband's study,
Smoking through her gown of flame,
She fell, burning in his arms,
Enwrapping him in screams and flame.
Death brought forth the blackest dawn,
Her husband raged, then grew a beard
To hide the scars embedded in his face.
"She lived with fire, she died in flame,"
You whispered as we left the house.
"We burn, we perish, save for the ghosts
That speak our name."
And walking from the house in shadow,
We almost saw the bride of ashes,
Flaming through the curtained window,
Twisted like Venetian glass.

Shards

Leaving jars of glaze,
Indigo, rutile, you walk
Beneath a blending sky,
A maker of pots.
Behind you, like mountains
Diminishing in distance,
The magnificent illusions:
Power, choice, security,
Replaced by the blind child,
The snarl of marriage,
The crumbling foundation.
You saw your house shudder,
Crack, and leave you
Like pieces of a broken vase,
Veined shards from Mesopotamia.
Now mended, set firmly,
The vase holds—
Imperfect but true.

Sappho

Entering the land of strangeness,
Your hands can change my body,
Pretend my chest has breasts
And take me as you would a girl.
Stroke away my savage grace
And contain my instinct's rage.

If our spirits move as one,
If my heart can understand
The passions of your body,
Then release me from this
Iron bondage, take my strength
Before it breeds destruction.

Every man is born a stranger,
Learn to trust my unknown arms,
Bring your lips upon my wounds,
Only you can make me warm.

VI

Procession

By the table crowded with capsules,
Thermometers, cards with signatures
That once meant love, telephone numbers
That filled your pockets like
Crumpled roses, you chart the rise
And fall of fever, writing on
A shadowed page through empty hours
When no friend calls, as though
Familiarity carried plague
And by a look, a word or gesture,
They, too, would become another carrier
In that long procession without an end.

Avondale

At the cemetery's end,
Beyond the veined stones
Of Kern, Pautler, Forbeck,
The farmlands stretch.
Two hawks, high in the sun,
Dapple the fields with shadow,
While the sound of cicada, sizzling
Like the long fuse of summer,
Rises through the thick quilt
Of grass, and I, standing at
Death's silent edge,
The rows of graves behind,
The patchwork fields ahead,
Suddenly feel joined
With the gnawed bones below,
The tall trees beyond,
Their tops like islands,
Rising, summoning,
Stretching into
The bright distance.

The Old Lovers

When there was nothing left to give
Except a glance across the bed,
They knew their love was now complete,
That there was nothing to expect
From all they'd gathered through the years
And brought to this quiet moment,
And they realized the side effects
Of wounds inflicted with barbed words
Had finally disappeared.
How long their love-making always was!
The numbers of their digital clock
Have replaced the hands
They watched for years.
No matter—time moves,
Indifferent to delays,
Relentless through our numbered days.

Beached

The soft-pawed tide falls over his feet
And when he watches it withdraw
He wants to bend and catch it,
Hold it, keep it the way
He would keep his memory which has left him,
A tide that never returns.
He could stand for hours by the sea,
An old man with wisps of hair like smoke
Hallucinating about the whitecaps
That curve like the mustache he wore
In the life he cannot remember,
And when his daughter moves beside him,
When she takes his hand
As he once took hers on this sleeve of beach
Forty years ago, he asks if they can
Walk into the sea together, right now,
Until they reach the other side.

Last Love

When he covers her hand which is lying
On her lap with his large, heavy hand
And feels his body leaning toward her
On the bench in the nursing home garden,
He feels he is protecting her with his
Entire being that can stride before her,
Although he, like she, can only manage
A step without his walker and must wait
For help to rise from this bench where
He was gently placed in his ninetieth year
Which has brought him close to this woman
Whose delicate hand fits beneath his
Like a pea under a shell in the game
He played with his sister so many years ago.
And if he could speak he would tell her
How her hair, parted like white curtains,
Allows him to imagine that death is only
An opening in light which they can enter
Together, his hand still covering hers,
Though they have never spoken in the warm
Afternoons when he is placed beside her
Before returning to his separate room
Where he sits alone and tries to remember
What has passed miraculously between them.

Air-Conditioner

My wife stops during lovemaking.
I watch her rise: an aging body
Cutting through the sultry air
As she crosses the room, leans forward
With a dancer's unforgotten grace
To draw in the quick cooling air.
Like bolts her hot flashes strike,
Always on the verge of orgasm.
But in the quick cooling air,
In the rhythm of renewed passion,
She comes like a woman
Abandoned to the glacial beauty
Of an arctic dawn, while I,
Looking at her in the light,
Consider how irrelevant
Her changed body has become.

Blessing

Your naked body reminds me
Of a white lily with long,
Curving petals that collect
The sunlight and the rain.
When my tongue enters you
I feel stripped of disguises
And leave my thoughts
Like a snake slipping out
Of its wrinkled skin.
Look, now, in the garden,
Past the lilies
Borrowed from flame,
Where the ruby throated
Hummingbird hovers over
A blossom that receives it,
The stem bowing for a blessing.

The Joyful Dark

When they lie down in the sunlight,
Naked in the field surrounded
By a shield of wheat,
He touches her with his tongue
That travels toward the paradise
She urges him to enter.
Old man, adulterer,
He renews himself in her
Young, vibrant body.
I will never know this renewal.
My wife joins me in the joyful dark,
Our bodies old, our paradise ever new.
We touch again with our fingers
What we have learned to see,
Sinking into the hollow
Of our mattress as we feel
Something like a sun
Growing warm inside us.

The Journey

We look back and consider how we arrived.
It was never mere sex but getting beyond it,
Getting beyond your vagina's ageless dance
As the marriage lasted despite our natural
Opposition, our need to be alone, to reclaim
Solitude and resist the intervention of another.

I wanted us to be joined in a place beyond
Our lust, beyond my cock rising at your touch,
Beyond your nipples unsettling the air,
Beyond what attracted us so passionately
With an aura that roused our sleeping selves
But would not endure until love embraced it.

And now we have come to a hill's smooth crest
With no one around us and dusk coming on.
The gulls drift out, drift out to sea
Without a message to decipher in the dark.
We have become what we always were,
Travelers standing together, travelers drawn apart.

The Robert McGovern Publication Prize is awarded to poets over 40 years of age who have published no more than one book. The prize is established in memory of Robert McGovern, poet, professor, co-founder of the Ashland Poetry Press, and long-time chair of the English Department at Ashland University. Manuscripts are submitted by nomination. The McGovern nominating panel currently consists of Alice Fulton, Andrew Hudgins, Philip Levine, Robert Phillips, Eamon Grennan, William Heyen, John Kinsella, Annie Finch, Carolyn Forché, Vern Rutsala, Richard Jackson, Gregory Wolfe and Gerry LaFemina. Ashland Poetry Press Editors also occasionally make an "Editor's Choice" selection for the McGovern series, outside of the regular nomination process.

Winners of the McGovern Prize are as follows:

Michael Miller, for *The Joyful Dark* (Editor's Choice, selected
   by Stephen Haven)
Maria Terrone, for *A Secret Room in Fall* (nominated by
   Gerry LaFemina)
Nathalie Anderson, for *Crawlers* (nominated by
   Eamon Grennan)
A.V. Christie, for *The Housing* (nominated by
   Eamon Grennan)
Jerry Harp, for *Gatherings* (nominated by John Kinsella)